images
for
radical
politics
vanessa
jimenez
gabb

RESCUE PRESS
CHICAGO, CLEVELAND, IOWA CITY

Design by Sevy Perez
Helvetica & Adobe Caslon Pro
rescuepress.co

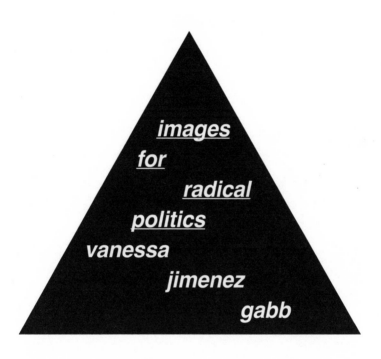

images
for
radical
politics
vanessa
jimenez
gabb

for my parents

images for radical politics

1

2

*The most revolutionary thing one can do
is always to proclaim loudly what is happening.*

ROSA LUXEMBURG

1

Economic Update

Working class wages have risen by five to six percent in China,
where billionaires exist more than anywhere else, but this is not
enough to offset the decline in wages for the American working class.

When I got out of bed, it was spring but not spring, most of the ice
gone back into the air, changing in ways that scare some of us.

The baguette, the fruit, the sausage came to me when I ordered them.

I had nowhere to be then. A whole blue sky and I didn't leave for
the blue sky.

Naked, I did as many burpees as I could in seven minutes and still
with nowhere to be then, with little breath to be.

Governor Scott Walker proposed to cut the budget of state universities in
Wisconsin by 300 million dollars, to change higher education from a way
to understand the world and talk about it with the people around you, to
vocational training. Also in higher education news, Purdue University
is offering students a new option to pay for their education: they can find
an investor to pay for their education in exchange for a percentage of their
future income.

It felt good to say let's buy something to eat and eat it in the park.

After you read something, it either stays with you or it doesn't.

I read a thirty-eight-page-long poem from beginning to end and understood that I needed to read more to understand it more, but I became more and more hands and feet in the 600 square feet of this apartment and the morning glory through the window.

Austrian central banking group Hypo Alpe Adria, a major lender in the middle of Europe, revealed it was short by ten billion euros. They have no money. The government of Austria bailed out this bank to the tune of one million euros; one state of Austria, Carinthia, guaranteed nine billion euros in loans, despite its annual revenue of two billion euros. Among the creditors that Carinthia will not be able to pay are several large banks in Germany. Hypo Alpe Adria made huge amounts of homeowner loans in southeastern Europe. The people are in trouble and can't pay back the mortgages, which means they can't pay the bank, which means the bank has no money to pay back the people it borrowed from to get the money it lent to the homeowners.

It feels unbearable to reiterate.

To know what is needed is to become and how to become and to find new reasons to become and what if we don't become together?

This and five tacos and two margaritas for $24 have brought me to a surprisingly well-lit basement in a church by the park, where, at the entrance, a man introduces himself as William and says the man giving the talk is a liberal. He believes in improvement.

Ten percent of the people own ninety percent of the wealth and the internal logic says they have always sought out and continue to seek out the hinterlands.

People come on the second Wednesday of every month to this basement in this church, to fill the seats, to be filled.

We are almost a sea.

Someone in the back is beginning to record and we are silencing and the almost sea is waiting to become the sea.

After

I say I remember
A woman
Sister says no
A man
Looked like a woman
No Mother says
Off the highway Father
Says no the park

Sirens
I don't recall sirens
They say an ambulance
And yes yes it was
After a road

A wandering into
From the bush
This woman
Or man
Really we had seen what
Was left of the person

To cover the part of the body
Missing the other parts
Wrist hand fingers
Must have lain somewhere
Hacked off in the green

There must have been
An open mouth
Screams
I don't remember
Blood nerves tendons
The act of violence
The inside of the body
I was small I saw color

And with no sound
A lot of white and pink somebody cut up
I tell you
What I told them

My Father and I Build a Family Tree

he names dead people
        as far back as two hundred years

he or she would have remembered
        more, he says

it is not morbid his saying
        this i want to get it

all, i say
        in case you are hit by a car tomorrow

this is morbid
        i like the way it feels

to see the blood
        the tiny red bugs

crossing over
        i smear

neither white nor black
        just alive a moment ago

his eyes a little wet
        allergy in the body

who gave this away before before
        is it Caribbean

to be intolerant
        is it indigenous to be intolerant

human to be of flowers and dust
        sent into the air

this is either very glorious
        or too ceremonial

i have never asked this
        many closed-ended questions

i hope it doesn't feel punitive
        to know without sounding

so imperious i am sorry
        something has opened

into more and i am here
        thinking of all the parts of me

that died at the bottom of a long night
        working and if not working

for the government making it work
        in one room

the beginnings of ism
        or ism

how well can we know ourselves
        in different systems of being

question answer parenthetical
        he comes upon a bit of memory

i put it in the blanks the men and women
        this is how i will place them

and remember them
        if there is a blank

it will go on forever
        far enough into the ghosts

all the fucking
        everyone did is in

our hair
        the air about us

to be here in the backyard alive
        spread like leaves

like buccaneers
        pilferers in the rainforest

The Robbers

Were at our door
I heard them
Trying to undo the chain
I remember waking and a hand
My heart wild
We ran to it
Punched it until it went away

The robbers were really one
Of our neighbors
So faded
This apartment for his
Doors say stay out
This is mine
Don't come up in here I'll kill you
Neighbor I don't know you like that
The cops are on their way
We might say

In another world
This would not be the poem
In another world there would be another way
To evoke pathos

Come closer
Let me see your face
Tell me your name
What has happened to you
Today what was taken
A woman
A man
A child
A job
A house
Make me understand
What you are looking for

Flatlands

for Canarsie

I.

we aren't far from the pier
years and years the grey pier
the pier is grey matter
isn't far from the brain
the spine
this is nice
you with me going
toward there
do you dream
i think i dream
about invisible places
i don't know
everyone is gone
this is what happens
sociologically
isn't all memory elegy
how do you know
it is improvidence
when you ask questions
you can answer

you punch a boy in the face
and you know
it was the only thing to do
you wanted to be fearless
and so you were

i am dizzy out on the highway
i want the only pizza
i have ever loved

2.
the mother and father tell the children
about their world
they talk about what it was like to have this
life they once had

they say years ago so much of everything was red
red our hearts
red our fists
for a few years war waged
we set fire to a great many places
and for a moment things looked promising

there is a way to reinvent
to mask the bad
to make the people react
against themselves and like that
the war continued
but it was over
humans executed

they say we are like spies now
we've gone underground
and you, you are the new agents of change

when will the conditions be such again for another war
the child asks
will we come out of hiding

it cannot help itself
so brazen sometimes
and those times are the times when it is hard
to look away
don't look away from us they beg
these are crisis moments
these you can see

but make no mistake, they say,
the conditions are always there
waiting for you to realize them
they are a serpent in the still of the night
coming way before it sinks its teeth
into your skin

3.
oh no, why you wan fuh go bak deh gyal

alma's son was shot in the mout
the bullet went right tru
missing man
the palate
everyting
dis was a church man yes
all he did was da church
he jus happen to be walkin by
kids
no he wasn't nuh kid

deh's nobody to sue
nobody has nothing gyal
i don't know
deh rich people dem
probably up in Ladyville deh
probably behind da gates
by Ladyville deh

if you wan fuh go weh deh tourists
sure deh have protection
or up by Chetumal deh
it's bad, gyal

Family Dinner

Gyal	They call
Gyal	They are calling
The vowels are	The vowels they are
The food of voice	Here a sorcery
This accent they tell me is	A dirt road in the Caribbean
Walk down for years	Don't leave
When built upon	Again and again
Don't leave	They sing eat
Yuh maga gyal eat	Black soup with boiled egg
With your lips	The sand sound

Girl in Placencia

Cool in my head
She so still
In the sea grape tree

What will happen
To her I thought
When she wandered away
She wandered over
From the somewhere part

Of the sand
She said neighbor
And named the parts of the land
And pointed and said we
Such brown
Little things

For that hour we flashed
To find that again

I would have to ask the people
What was she
Called and is she

The cabana is
There on the site
The veranda below the blue
If they know they will say
Yes she has been in the states
Or down in the sea

At the Bar

There is a wedding
If you look past the football on television
You can see the white
Of the bride's dress
A mermaid dress
A snow queen
And the black water of her hair

The music loud and flooding
Into the music of this room
They say it's cheaper to do these things
On Sundays and it must be even less
To rent out one of the rooms beside others
Where people are foolish

The bride passing stops
The men slam each other
And sweat hard and hurt themselves and this
Mother squeals pointing her daughter to the long hair

To the lace
Of the dress as it passes in front
Isn't it an absolute dream
The girl mouth open
Looking out at the field

LBD

I wanted a little black dress
To be the dialectic
To be the poem
I wrote about cities
How every city is a city
Of contrasts
The living people
Are opposites
These are
Because the others are not
Everything is political
A little black dress
A woman
Saying no
Is a political act
Anything we say
And then mean
And hardly recover from
For some years
Hanging black
After black

At the Gym

My hair needs washing
I am oily at the root
Petulant with bad waves
Relax
Bring your ass
To your ankles
Ian says
I can't
I scream
I can't I stop being
Happy just like that
On account of my hair
Looking crazy
That and my belly
Showing out

When I'm alone here
It's just me
The weights are alone
I don't challenge their aloneness
I watch Netflix

I can't stop Netflix
It fucks the poetry out
All the harlequin dramas
The he waiting for seasons
For the her
The me
Watching the them back when
It's not you
It's me they say

I say
Like shit I haven't been
Operating as someone else
I've been exactly me
Coming and going
Like I got it like that
I don't
Every part of me wants to
Bring my ass
To the machinery that confounds
That is change
The not knowing how to change
Half in love
With the body
Not knowing how

Xunantunich

You are in my mouth sweet when I hear Belize
Oh, my sweet Belize

On TV they are eating panadas
We ate panadas just this week
I fried them barefoot like a mother
Even though I am no mother
I was one once for eight weeks
Then we were in Belize

Remember the ruins
Xunantunich, the stone woman
We took a boat to land
To a bus that delivered us rum-drunk

Post-colonial
I didn't recall what fell from my uterus
We saw the sun and fried for days and tasted better

Photos of us exist somewhere
We were so there
The mosquitos took our blood

Skydeck Selfie

everyone out smiling
one another in the city up in a crack
binge last night out
on the ledge a real life
didn't move me
to say things like i don't know
like i know i don't know just
like i meant them but didn't
really mean all i brought with me

i say things just to hear them
outside my mouth
even if they mean
doesn't matter to me
i don't know whose film i think
i am in this fire
watching the history of Chicago's burning
watching a film
on the history of the burning
is watching myself burn and wait to be rebuilt

if they are going to make us watch this

they should tell the truth
there are children here lovers walking away
believing no one fell and no one fell
smashed red to come and not think
about exploitation
to think about exploitation and say this
this is what i think of and want to speak of
walk with me

Williams says love is unworldly and nothing comes of it but love
and nothing
stays in me more than the same person
for more than three thousand days
i have been the same
person for more than three thousand days
we are one hundred
stories the one hundred stories
revolutionary

this just ain't it this just ain't
i looked him dead and said nah
he said are you sure that's you
speaking are you
about tomorrow
i don't know i don't know i don't know

what does it mean to know anyhow
does it mean you have happened
to yourself unequivocally

have you ever tried
to let your body listen
have you ever
thought of changing your hair
what color would it be
if you didn't think i was that man
if you heard these words
before you started thinking
they were bad

i am trying to be no better than good
just good at knowing
what it really means to be me what does it
a woman on line with the tits i want
to have sex we haven't had since
we landed it's gone
my way for a while so i walk along
the top of this place so he can take photographs
and i can look at him and look

Aubade with Ham

i don't want you to spend all that money
i make you a sandwich right now
because i have everything i need
i don't know the next time i will have everything i need
we rarely have everything at once
there is no time to do anything
the way it needs to be done
in five minutes the road is going to be too crowded
to drive on and yet
the choice is not a choice really
there is the sandwich in your kitchen
one for lunch and then one
for you to forget
it will be about the future
you are asleep and i am awake
and so for me it is the future
all of these things i leave them for you in a bag
here, take the sandwich, please
here, it is a pound of meat
the pink sky and bread

Summer, 2014

i am here for the meeting
in the house by the sea
i am here to be with the others
things are happening
someone shouts
things been happening
someone shouts back
there is glimmer here
because there is truth
i think both statements are true
things are happening
and things been happening
they are like saying
there is revolution
and there is tyranny
they are like saying
we are ourselves
and we are nothing
like what we could be
if given the chance
here in the house by the sea
we are spontaneous

reacting to cold blood
knowing what needs to be done
trying to establish what we need
to get it done
the dining table an orchard
we set down what we have
we pick what we need
to know more of
so much green
more people come
listen to this
no listen to this
we want more
it is possible to transform
we fan out
some to the porch
some fill the bedrooms
we rotate through
everything that has been left to us
what is here is rich
all the others
who have gathered in this house
and labored over the many ways
we are and have been
we are and have

been working and working
day into night
for what is ours
for the whole thing
all of us in this house

Images for Radical Politics

East New York, Brooklyn, 1971

We have nothing to lose

This great feeling of love
Belonging not to then not to now
But to the future

This takes us
When they are ready to be taken

Everything makes sense
The moment it makes sense
Everything after is for life

Upper West Side, Manhattan, 1955

The mother says to the daughter
Blanco your dress
So very black
Your hair in summer

Words shutter
Like shells windblown
In verano
My hands' color
Then yours
This sound
Hum of the Ford
The waves this way

Crown Heights, Brooklyn, 1963

Here we have the yard
An extension of the house
(A material representation)
The land of women
Brought from the Caribbean
To the street named
For Mark the Evangelist
It is important to note that
Children here are children
Of the kin-group

Belize City, Belize, 1961

Hurricane Hattie is lethal
The water rises up
All of the little houses are built on stilts
To save themselves from the land
Coming through
Taking itself back

The Treaty of Versailles
Said yes cut away everything
Between this river and that
Take all the mahogany you can carry
Until there is none left
Take with you
All the open that was

East New York, Brooklyn, 1972

He reads of the countryside as the beginning

A history of kings
Coming to their centers
And producers now called tenants

And lords compelling tenants
Unfixed by legal or customary standard
Fixed by the wind through the market

Cooperation is something
In the darkness the petty proprietor shoots up
The petty proprietor is a precondition

Who then would lead what needed leading
Resistance is what it is called when it is needed
The same way not needing cannot be helped
The way what is meant by land is not yet work
But the preparation of it to be worked

Upper West Side, Manhattan, 1963

They recite the water together
Capitals given the bodies
The father-daughter country
Is all the geography of the world
The body as beginning
And endless

Somewhere one day
She cannot follow

Crown Heights, Brooklyn, 1968

Even to the one
Who back home is said to have
The powers that make structures
Appear in barren fields
Flying objects come down
Where he wants them

Even to him
The stars here
Standing there burning
Are nothing
More than stars

Belize City, Belize, 1981

When a father

Is returned to the dirt
By his son
The story of the father
Returns to the son
And the son will return it

To his own daughter
She will be
The mother of the story

East New York, Brooklyn, 1983

She plays the piano in the middle room
Of the railroad apartment
He has flown back
Across the blue
To study the economics
Of his small enfeebled country
The word is how strange
They are to not believe in God
Her belly growing as they speak strangely
We all came from the sea
We are foaming
But do not have to foam

2

Institution

Don't get married. A great love does not exist without protest,
my mother told me, have a beautiful run without law, with
protest!

Organdy from birth, with a godless belief in the system of things,
in search of some twin being, a diadem in your mouth, you were
named protest.

I named you and you went, taking extremities into you for
decryption, opening into wheat fields, your hands passing along
without protest.

Everything that passes for voyage is us awash in injustice, mortal,
mortal, being young we bleed, loving nothing more than protest.

What could be more legitimate than an idea between us,
fatal or not, here or not, time must pass and so we must protest.

A love poem begins with hazard somehow, the concept of time,
a cloud calling itself gas, only that, and I calling that protest.

The Lady of Civilization

after Friedrich Engels's *The Origin of the Family, Private Property, and the State*

No house, I have
today
I have a far-off reality
as do you
we were savage
before we were barbarian
anthropologists say
and economists
I can say
I have a memory
of an opening
of walking
into another epoch
but not a belief in it
this is called civilization
ask me
where I am
and I will
ask you for the answer
what have we done?

us but all of us
what could our love have been
if not born
from 18th-century enlightenment
I could have been
a forest
a mother
among the Iroquois Seneca
a great clanswoman
before the herds
of horses
sheep and pigs
bred by the Euphrates
with milk and meat
rapidly men augment
and learn
a more advanced application
of work and property
men obtained food
and so the instruments
of work
the division of labor
our division of labor
being what it was
we worked so hard

didn't we
I believe we did
in our ways
but where
is the knowledge of this
wealth increased
matriarchal law of inheritance
was overthrown
but we have no knowledge
of this either
the overthrow
of mother-right was the world
historical defeat
of the female sex
all things were turned
into commodity

*

you brought to me
the word marriage
and I asked what that meant
if history meant
I was unfree
how found
would we be
I wanted you to know
I want to be
a woman
I wanted you to know
I have always been
preoccupied by this
though you were
not and so were we
doomed to know
each other well
enough to say goodbye
or maybe
we came to know
nothing about each other
not even how
to say yes
just as I will

sense my own fear
with strange men
the way the world works
its terror so
that I will
know you
suddenly in them
the contradictions live
in us
in cellular form
I am not entirely
without a place
to live yesterday
I fed our cats
then lay back
in your bed
I imagined
falling asleep
if you had
found me
waiting to be discovered
because I want to be
discovered
look
I have told you far more

now than ever then
about passion
passion:
the first form
of rapture
remembered
by the poets
of the Middle Ages
writing about knights
lying beside wives
of other men
it is a long way to this
I have
I am here
a winter
of me and me

*

this frightening
those twelve years
a long time
to do anything
to be someone
where do people begin
and end
in that
we were in Chicago
just two weeks before
we were side-swept
by another car
shooting like a star
I swear how
is it that time passes
without us
ever being side-swept
that time passes
without us having
every single thing
happen to us
you should go
the driver said
go now

this is not mine
I shouldn't be here
yet I saw myself here
endangered or not
I saw myself here
here
where
I am I more
than I was
it has been
about longing
for a future
which is a past
ruthless existence
stay back
you say to yourself
you are always
about to die

*

The communistic household, in which most or all of the women belong to one and the same gens, while the men come from various gentes, is the material foundation of that supremacy of the women which was general in primitive times, and which it is Bachofen's third great merit to have discovered. The reports of travelers and missionaries, I may add, to the effect that women among savages and barbarians are overburdened with work in no way contradict what has been said. The division of labor between the two sexes is determined by quite other causes than by the position of woman in society. Among peoples where the women have to work far harder than we think suitable, there is often much more real respect for women than among our Europeans. The lady of civilization, surrounded by false homage and estranged from all real work, has an infinitely lower social position than the hard-working woman of barbarism, who was regarded among her people as a real lady (lady, frowa, Frau—mistress) and who was also a lady in character.

*

my human mind
stands bewildered
by things
of which we are capable
I wake
every morning
and go to work
and other places
the difference
between now and then
is that I am without
you
that is clear
but not always
true
some days
the day is a lie
yesterday the morning
sky appeared to me
but it was the smoke
from a factory
where people had been
at work
hours already

I wanted to tell
you of skies
I saw and talk
with you about
what made them
that way
and how even humans
might change them
as you may have
wanted to tell me
many things
that you became
vast because of
impoverished
because of
but never did
because
that is how
you continued
without me
and I continued
without you
even when
we were
there together

we did
all of that
ourselves
the morning
and the evening
the year
measured by
the retreat
our own vastness
our own poverty
our own sky
owners of
these things
as if
we could own them

*

that evening I drove
and drove
until I reached
a mountain town
I parked
and spent money
at an apothecary
on oils
masks
a candle
named Serenity
people had settled
there many years
before and after
had manufactured things
that dirtied the marsh
nothing left
of what it was
it wasn't snowing
but it felt like it
could be somewhere
nearly another
another state maybe
miles for miles

of water

or ice

and woods

mountains

like that very one

and it was

almost the same white

and then I drove home.

Animalia

an elephant calf doesn't know
how to use her trunk
her truth
what it means to balance

actual combat leads to wounds
death possibly
the hippos know this
bone-dry
relentlessly hot
not concerned with the heat

and then, rain
the river divides again and again

what life has the river given
we have lived under the spell of the river
it has defined cultures
life itself

everyone is here in a river
of shit
the flies stuck to our faces

men move a barge across the river
in the oppressive heat
the village moves with the river
the king and queen
when they set foot on the land is when
they all will have arrived

fuck the king and queen
on the backs of mammals

concern ourselves with the heat
raise dust
realize we are lions

we travel 2,000 miles
we travel across the bridges
we want mangroves
we want to preen ourselves

i would like to go to Africa
i would like to be shot into space
the wild dogs
make everyone go the night without

river always river reinvented
the people will move the river
somewhere it has never been

A Most Violent Year

deer at the end of a field

can't come up with cash

the truck driver at the end of a field

can't come up with cash

the soul divided

beyond the Industrial Age

the deer the driver

the bank the anonymous gunman

eat the deer

eat the driver

this is deferential treatment

the mansion is good

deregulation good and lawless

a reasonable way of business

studies in confinement and compression

dear deer dear driver

how do you rise

how do you not rise

the panic is inevitable

but you are inevitable

the field is morality

not the mansion and the silver tongue

the fleet of driver and deer is inevitable

speak not the coupe

but the driver

the panic that starts the night

now the rise now

the crumbling walls now

the dock now

the trade now

the company now

the field

Relax Melodies

The waves crashing
Through my phone
My budget vacation
This close
To a holodeck
Except it's Brooklyn
It is the future

Capitalists don't fear
Commoners they fear
Other capitalists
So all these gadgets
Can be mine
Until I can't keep up
Because they will begin
To bite off each other
And everything will atrophy
I think of when we loved
An innovation like AOL
A Timbaland beat
Was a beautiful thing
We named ourselves

To be hardcore
In that sort of box
You be boy I'll be girl
We used to say
When will you appear
In my face so spectral
So we can
Bump fantasy back and forth
Are you away like it says you are
Ok so you're never coming back
Aren't you
Such a tough guy
In that camouflage
Color font

I don't have the time
I need to sort this out
These divisions of labor
Got me tripping
When you don't type back
I bifurcate into a princess
And a douche bag
You say when I'm on
So much I'm not even
Here

In West New York, NJ

the homegirls are brunch-drunk
are tigers in the freezing
the water all the lights
in the water the sky
a skyline in their pockets

they want so much
to get on the other side
of the city in through the tunnel
fall like Alice and grow to curse
the tyranny of the clock
they curse their office buildings

can we not do something else
with our lives besides this
like kill birds
there's something in the black cold
makes them want to slap someone

Raise

I need a safe house everywhere I go.

The invasions are every day.

I have to spend more time than I have, thinking about asking
for more.

If and when, might and exactly how much, having everything
before me, my life.

In the summer, I don't drive much, I don't use the city's roads or
tunnels or bridges. I can work another job, for another employer.

The fall, the winter, the spring, the little car my silver pod.
I become more proprietary. This is mine and this is yours.

All year, the day, inherently overtime. After a certain point,
I produce more than I am given.

All year, I am a thing.
All year, I am salt.

I am not afraid to talk about money. Liberating to hear you say
this is nothing strange to me. I understand the beauty of our labor.

Liberating to hear my sister say she is looking into different
modes of representation.

Liberating to hear my father and mother say this is what it
means to be on an exalted mission. This is what it means to know
yourself.

There is nothing unsafe left to talk about.

This grand and that grand are what I am. But I had no say in that.

And there is not enough more they'd be willing to give before
this would become another this altogether.

Log: Christine

8:50 — Arrive/turn on, try to beat boss make it seem like I got in before her, so I could leave earlyish each day.

9 — Fill up water bottle, eat breakfast (bowl of company-provided cereal or a banana). Talk in kitchen about work gossip. Complain a lot. Talk to people I don't know that well about dumb fucking shit, like weather, company projects, breakfast, or lunch. Sometimes about online dating. A lot of ppl like to talk about it.

9–11 — Facebook, IM, send work emails, read work emails, Facebook, IM, IM, IM, think about snacks, get snack, send more work emails, work (no more than fifty minutes total) on one big editorial piece. Maybe make a phone call to a writer or blogger about future piece. Chit-chat (in OPEN WORKSPACE where I sit ONE FOOT FROM MY BOSS), share funny links. Pretend to work. Read about PhD programs, fellowships, check Submittable. Lots of Twitter.

11–12 — Take a fucking break. Sitting that long is a bummer. Get up and take laps around the building. See work friends, sit around and chat, take my computer with me so it looks like I'm working on a big project or a collaboration. Sit on outside patio and call my mom. Think about which food truck I am going to spend fifteen bucks on lunch. Get back to desk by 11:30 and pretend work again until 12:10.

12:10-ish — Long lunch with work besties. Talk about how stupid work is. How we all want to quit. How we are fat. We talk about our future weddings. We talk about which guys we'd wanna fuck at work if we had to pick. We talk about which old guys are hot. More online dating talk with single coworkers.

1–3 — Meetings. On and off. Super boring and never informative—usually it's announcements that don't directly affect me. Or it's bad meetings about how the company is doing poorly. Sometimes it's a pitch meeting, where I only pretend to participate. I bring my laptop to meetings—to pretend I'm working. I'm IM'ing. Facebooking. Tweeting. Submitting fiction. Making fiction notes about asshole coworkers. Everyone talks too much—all the meetings run over. Sit back at desk and try to finish tasks in between meetings, but there are so many meetings, so nothing really gets done.

3 — Take break and walk outside. Walk around office. Eat leftover treats from birthdays. Sit at desk and try to get easy tasks finally done so I can focus on personal things.

5 — Start wrapping up, make sure the lame shitty tasks and correspondence are actually completed for the day. Overall, I remind myself that the entirety of my job is about 1–3pm of real work a day.

5–6 — Watch clock. Hope boss leaves early. Prepare for boss weekly 1:1 where I say how busy I am. Hate self for selling soul to work at a terrible editorial outlet that has no backbone and is run by fuckers who only care about money. Stand outside and wait for ride home—make more personal calls.

I make 75k per year on salary and I know it's weird to work it out by hour cuz of payroll weeks?—that's including bonus and commuter benefit. I am salary so I get medical, dental, eye, and chiropractor coverage too. And I get four weeks paid vacay, plus ten sick days, plus two personal, plus holiday pay.

Log: Mike

* Left work at 12 AM.
* Waited for bus until 12:30 AM
* Exited bus at 1:12 AM
* Waited for second bus to arrive at approx 1:17 AM
* Arrived home at 1:30 AM
* Sat in living room staring off into space until 1:38 AM
* Went to bed
* Woke up at 7:45 AM
* Showered/brushed teeth
* Got a glass of water
* Sat with glass of water in front of TV and watched the news for 10–15 minutes.
* Bus arrived at 8:30ish
* Exited bus to catch second bus at 9 AM
* Arrived for 11 AM–12 AM shift at 10:13
* Take hour lunch at 4 PM
* Off work at 12 AM
* Rinse and repeat.

Base wage is 17.50 with 16 OT hours built into my schedule, and on those hours I make 25 an hr.

Log: Heather

Every day, I walk the wind tunnel that is the six long blocks to
the F, then ride an hour into work. My day consists of building
"logs," which are like playlists for a given twenty-four-hour pe-
riod. I need to schedule everything that will happen on-air for
our channel within a twenty-four-hour period. I share this work
load with two others, so while I'm working on Monday's log,
someone is working on Tuesday, and a third person is working
on Wednesday, and so on.

The log comes to me completely empty—only placeholders
where the films/programs go, and I see blank spaces where all
the breaks are (commercial breaks). It's my job to sift through
the thousands of promos in our inventory and add them to my
bin to choose from, so I can select appropriate ones to add in
the blank spots. "'Unfaithful'—tonight at 7 pm" promo will go
here, and look, I have thirty seconds left to fill, so I will add a
thirty-second promo after that—"All-new 'Rectify,' Thursday
at 10 pm." I choose to put the "Unfaithful" promo first, because
the film will air tonight; whereas "Rectify" will air Thursday, a
few days later. I also choose to put those two promos together
because one is a promo for a film, the other is a promo for a
show—it adds variety.

May seem creative, but most of the time, it's a lot of clicking and dragging, clicking and dragging. Sometimes we only have 3–4 shows/films to promote, so it's a lot of cycling through the same promos, clicking on them, dragging them from the bin and into the empty slots on the log/playlist.

Then there are the snipes—those little graphics that come up periodically at the bottom of the screen that say, "All-new 'Face Off,' Tuesday at 9"—it has the same messaging as a promo, but instead of it airing for thirty seconds during a commercial break, you just see the graphic during the program you're watching. These are especially boring because they have the SAME formula. Every program has segments. For example, "Unfaithful," a two-hour film, may be broken up into eight segments. We choose to air snipes twice in each segment. So that is sixteen snipes just for one film. And here is how we determine when the snipes will appear—we want them to pop up fifteen seconds after the START of a segment, and the second snipe will pop up forty-five seconds from the END of the segment. It's that simple. So I have an area on the log where I indicate those times (00:15 and −00:45), for EVERY segment, of EVERY film. (Of course we have exceptions, like if a film has subtitles, we choose not to air snipes.) But for the entirety of a given twenty-four-hour log, I have to copy and paste 00:15 and −00:45 next to every snipe in every film. This is where carpal tunnel meets boredom.

I have at least five meetings per week, only 1–2 of which pertain to me. The rest, I just have to look like I'm paying attention.

Then I have to assign codes for every element, every promo (all versions of it—Tuesday, next Tuesday, tomorrow, next, thirty-second versions, fifteen-second versions, and so on), and assign codes for all the snipes. No two codes can ever repeat, or there will be mayhem.

Log: Miguel

9:00 — Downtown Brooklyn. Few areas exemplify the changes
in the borough more (maybe Williamsburg). Whenever I'm here,
I think about that Diddy show—"Making the Band." Remember
this?? Well, one episode they make the cast walk over the Brooklyn
Bridge and get Junior's cheesecake. Like, that was Brooklyn's image
to the world. Cheesecake, the Bridge, Nathan's. Now nobody gives
a fuck about the cheesecake. If someone visits you in Brooklyn, you
don't automatically think, "Yo, you have to try this cheesecake—this
is our thing!" Our things either just don't matter anymore or are
being replaced with their things. ANYWAY—I go to Bond Street for
a hearing at the Environmental Control Board regarding fines for
a property. Common occurrence, maybe once every three months.
Sometimes they're dismissed, but usually not. One of the reasons
behind New York's rising rents: the city is making bank off land-
lords, and most landlords in turn pass the costs on to their tenants.
The room is packed. I'm probably here on the average side of what
people have come to hope to avoid paying—$10,000. And not all
landlords are these large billion-dollar corps. We're decent enough
in size where it's ok, but you get someone who is dependent on one
or two small rental properties having to pay $10k on one fine and
that one bedroom apartment they were happy to rent out for $1,500
because the tenant was nice just went up to $1,800 next year.

11:00 — In Sunset Park. Talk to lawyer about a couple of evictions; go over a new statement with a tenant who we had to take to court last week for a few months past due rent; review some plans from a new commercial tenant's architect.

12:30 — Lunch/watch reality home improvement shows cause they're sort of related to what we do and so easier to justify watching.

12:45 — Run to get food for our office mascots—koi fish.

1:00 — Deal w people calling for apartments, tenants calling about all sorts of problems, respond to a few emails. Visit manager at local bank about looking into some foreclosures available to buy. We never buy foreclosures. Prices in NYC are so insane; however, there are few alternatives for sensible deals. At least until the next crash coming any day now...

2:00 — Bring one of our construction crew to an apartment we're renovating and check progress.

2:45 — Talk with local Business Improvement District about joining their Board of Directors. Seems like some interesting civic work without too onerous a time commitment, so I join.

3:15 — Pick up some materials for renovation project at another property.

3:45 — Bay Ridge. Go to project site, bring materials, check progress.

4:30 — Head home.

Log: Frank

6:30 — get to job, change clothes, have coffee.

7:00 — start work; get tools, work plans, materials, and ladders to exact job area.

9:15 — coffee break.

9:15 — back to work.

12:00 — lunch.

12:30 — back to work.

2:00 — start to pack up tools, ladders, and materials; lock them up.

2:15 — wash up, change clothes, leave job.

All of the accomplishment comes when the total job is finished, tested, and turned over to the owner or client.

All of the entertainment and everyday good feelings are provided by my imagination.

Log: Sam

7:30am — Wake up, shower, and do my hair and makeup. My hair is naturally wavy so I typically straighten it. For makeup, I keep it pretty simple—black eyeliner, mascara, and lip balm.

8:30am — Leave Royal Garden Hotel and walk through Kensington Gardens to HQ. Usually stopping along the way for a caramel mocha iced coffee. I don't typically drink coffee but to avoid the time difference hitting me midday, I'll grab one to kick-start my day.

9:00am — Yesterday was the first day of market as the product management team walked us through the new collection. We had first seen it the other night at the fashion show but now we get the chance to touch and feel and really play with it. There are quite a few regions here at HQ because I work for a global company. The agenda allots a certain amount of time for each region to sit with a product category and begin to assort for their region. Before we start, I usually spend the first ten minutes checking and answering email. I'll also re-review sales analysis based on season, style, color, silhouette, price point, etc, to get an understanding of what did and did not resonate with our customers the prior season.

9:30am to 11:30am — Womenswear is first. It's my favorite category. It tells the story; it connects the dots between all the other product categories—accessories (bags/wallets), soft accessories (scarves), footwear, and jewelry. We are introduced to our fit model for today's session. We do a quick first pass of what we think would be best for our woman. We usually have the fit model try on everything so we can take photos of each look, this way we can review it later if we need to. In addition, either myself or someone else on the team will also try on the clothing to get an idea of how it will look on a "real" woman. At the same time, we are reviewing the looks that went down the runway, as well as when it is expected to arrive in stores. We need to be sensitive to any looks that we absolutely must have to make sure that the inspiration and feel of the collection trickle down to our stores and ultimately our customers.

11:30am to 12:00pm — Soft accessories. Scarves, hats, and gloves. This one goes pretty fast as the offering is small. We usually pick up the essentials that our customers know us for and that are season-appropriate. In addition, we will pick up any colors and/or prints that help tie together the collection.

12:00pm to 1:00pm — Lunch. We have the same selection all week and I look forward to it each day. Three types of salad—I always get the arugula, tomato, and mozzarella; two types of quiche—I always get the roasted pepper and feta; multiple types of wraps—I always get the chicken caesar; and always one chocolate chip cookie. I love sweets. I am a strong believer in consistency and organization.

1:00pm to 2:30pm — Footwear. Always a favorite amongst women because your feet are always the same size regardless if you lose or gain weight. Because of this, it has the ability to instantly make you feel more confident, more beautiful, more powerful. There are so many choices and it is a great thing. You want this dilemma. We have everyone in the group try on different styles to see how it looks and most importantly, how it feels. Is it comfortable? How is the pitch? Walk around the showroom. A few times.

2:30pm to 5:00pm — Accessories Part 1. The biggest part of the business and can also be the trickiest. It is another category that is "no size" and has the power to make you feel all types of ways. Everyone is loving this collection and that is music to my ears. You want that. You need that. Shopping is a highly emotional experience. There is always the need, function, practicality but how it makes you feel overpowers any of that. Even more so at this price point. It is luxury. Personally, I have fallen for the structured camera bag in burgundy. Everything about it is just right—the size, the color, the saturation, the hardware, even the price. I am thinking about how I will wear this bag and how long until it will be in stores so I can buy it for myself.

5:00pm to 6:30pm — Meeting 1. The buyers from each region meet to discuss their initial thoughts on the collection, what they like and don't like and ultimately, what will drive their businesses. It is easy to get lost in the fantasy of it and the journey it can take you on. I mean, that is what I love most about it. But it is a business nonetheless, and the end result must be profit.

6:30pm — We walk back to the hotel. Go back to your room, put your stuff down, maybe even change your outfit. Call an Uber.

7:30pm to 9:30pm — Dinner at a trendy London restaurant. I am falling asleep. The food is amazing. I always order one drink but barely drink it. I need to be completely present and on it because our time is very limited in London. Besides, I will be working when I get back to my room.

10pm to 11pm — Checking and answering emails. It is 5pm in NY after all. Working through today's notes.

11pm to 12am — Get ready for bed. Watch Netflix. Say good-night to my boo in NY.

Day 2 over.

Log: Sara

8 — Incoming texts from a very anxious case manager based at the middle school program about his laptop not turning on and it contains the program's primary database and his documentation. Ask CM to remain calm and inform him "I'm on my way" to school and pick us up some coffee.

9 — Arrive at middle school; greet and check in with security guard about how things are going. She smiles and says ok. Inquire about safety issues this wk. Whole demeanor changes and suddenly goes right into how the entire week there have been fights, safety issues between two ethnic groups at the school; conflicts are escalating and now adults and older siblings are becoming involved with knives and bats. They don't have enough safety coverage support. Concerns for today: it's Friday and warm. Students are more restless. Warmer weather brings more problems.

9:05 — Enter the family resource room where two staff members are housed along with a school program director.

9:10 — Connect with program director and request an update on escalating school conflicts, safety and mediation efforts along with notified parties. Request to meet with principal if possible. Following up also on an email sent out earlier in the week. Make final recommendations on current school climate that include a safety plan and updating staff and students. Move on to discuss audit readiness for program director. Discuss a school event that the clinic will participate in to cover and promote mental health topics to staff, parents, and students.

9:20 — Check phone. Texts and missed calls from the clinic team. Call clinic to provide guidance.

9:40 — Check CM laptop. Attempt problem unsuccessfully. Review school conditions and briefly make a temporary safety plan and review exit strategies at school.

9:50 — Stand up to check on an irate teacher cursing and yelling in open family resource space regarding how money was stolen from her. She is flailing around screaming and storms out followed by security guard and parent coordinator. She is heading to find students who she believes stole from her.

9:51 — Talk to CM and family worker and ask if this type of outburst happens often. Yes it does. She is known for her outbursts.

9:55 — Briefly check in with director. Strongly advise her to notify her two supervisors of safety concerns at school so they are kept in the loop and don't find out by another source. To remind her they may offer support and guidance.

9:58 — Family comes in. PD informs me this family will be referred to clinic. The family's son has been threatened to be stabbed after school.

10 — Leave the school to take train back to Manhattan.

10:02 — Goodbye to a different security guard and also get a sense from him of being anxious on school's safety issues.

10:46 — Arrive in clinic and sit with school social worker who is at the clinic today covering another staff member on vacation. Debrief with her on school visit.

11 — Another admin director finds me to speak about school and next steps.

11:26 — Another program staff member asks for an update on school.

11:43 — Sitting at desk for first time. Make calls. Supervisor. Employee. New employee. HR.

12:30 — Left for lunch.

1:10 — Take call from supervisor to check in on program items.

2 — Spoke to HR about new hire.

2:30 — Submit an end-of-the-year online survey for a program that is due today.

3 — Emailed executive director to request a meeting with school. Open mail. Calls to hospitals to follow up on admitted clients.

3:23 — Met with intake coordinator to assign new cases.

3:30 — Prep Monday data; run reports and review productivity data collected for the week to date.

4 — Review calendar for the week. Invite consumer to IRC mtg on Monday.

4:14 — Remind team of payroll and Monday data.

4:20 — Meet with intake coordinator and make a plan to call families to assign to open therapy slots; phone calls and messages.

4:45 — Connect with client who is graduating from high school in a few weeks.

5 — Leave.

Annual Salary: 75k

Log: Anonymous

6:30
Wake up
Get out of bed
Try to get some feels in on my lady friend before she goes to work
Hopefully get a handful of that big ol' booty

7:00
Roll a joint
Smoke that joint
Pound a protein shake

8:00
Get on the train
Listen to music or edit mobile photos

8:45
Get to work
Respond to emails

9:00
Company meeting
Discuss fuck-ups and how not to fuck up

10:00
Reach out to CTOs and CEOs via email or LinkedIn messages

12:00
Leave work
Go to Just Salad and cop a salad
Ask myself why I am spending $10 on a salad

12:30
Get back to work
Eat the salad at my desk

Rest of Day
Speak to candidates or interview candidates and interview people
for my company
Schedule interviews for my candidates and clients the rest of the day

5:30
Bounce up out that bitch
Get back on the train
Try to get a good spot on the train so I can get a good view when I
am going over the bridge

6:30
Get to the gym, warm up, stretch, barbell warm-up, lift mad shit

9:00

Bounce up out that bitch

Go home and shower

Smoke on some tree

Try to get inside of her and go to sleep by 10:00

Most likely 11:00

Log: Ashleigh

Annual salary: roughly $55,000

6:40AM For once, I'm awake before Freya, who is two and who loves to "wake up in the darkness." Start the coffee, get dressed, take Freya to the bathroom. I spread avocado on toast while she sits across from me, licking peanut butter off her fingers. Dustin wakes up and the two of them begin to plan their day. Out the door at 7:52 7:55 8:01, Freya chasing after me and Dustin herding her back into the apartment and I'm half-running to make the train.

8:40AM I walk into my classroom and set out the little mats that help the kids stay put during circle time. Then I'm cutting out construction paper figures and refilling glue bottles and texting my mom who wants to say good morning.

9:00AM I can hear the kids in the hallway. I open the door. There is a small stampede. Tiny backpacks get hung on hooks.

9:50AM "It's clean up time, everybody / it's clean up time, everyone! / I'll help you / and you help me / and we'll have lots of fun!" This is the first time I'll sing this song today.

10:32AM The last student has left from the day's first class. Immediately I am scrolling through Facebook while taking strong pulls of coffee.

10:45AM By the time my second class begins, I'm feeling settled into the day. I can tell what didn't work in my earlier lessons, and I make little adjustments with this group. They get a better version of me than my first group of students do.

11:10AM *Why do you guys dump out every toy every single day? Oh my god, please stop shouting! Why are you chasing each other—you were just getting along! When is it clean up time? When can I go home?*

11:20AM *Oh my god, look at all your wiggly puppy bodies collapsing during "Ring Around the Rosie." You guys are the cutest. This is the best job.*

12:15PM I'm not hungry but I feel like rewarding myself for something, so I walk over to the deli and buy a bag of Goldfish. I eat them as I walk back to the classroom, and then I turn on KEXP and email all the parents whose kids were being especially wonderful or difficult. Fifteen minutes before lunch is over, I remember I wanted to use this time to stretch and draw, so I get out my sketchbook and sit in a straddle and start to make a comic about how I don't have time to do anything. The next class begins to assemble in the hall.

1:00PM My afternoon class is all three- and four-year-olds. They seem so sophisticated compared to my morning two-year-olds. *What must it be like to work with adults?*

1:18PM I text one student's nanny to ask where his snack is while dispersing hand sanitizer to sixteen germ-ridden little fingers.

1:35PM *You are much better artists than I am. You guys really get color theory. Why is any given four-year-old a better artist than I am? That can't be good. Well, that's why I didn't become a professional artist, I guess. But maybe I should have? Is it too late? Wait—don't eat that paint!*

2:42PM There are eighteen minutes left in this class and every minute seems to take an hour. I turn on some '50s R&B and get out scarves and instruments for the kids to play with. *Should I be doing some sort of music lesson right now? Wait, no, they're little kids. Just let them enjoy the music, the feel of the scarves in their hands, the weird rhythms they bang out on those cymbals.*

3:02PM Now the room is quiet again. I set out books for tomorrow's class and pack up my bag. I step into the elevator and go up to the thirty-third floor.

3:15PM In this apartment, so large my footsteps echo, live two of my students—bright and mischievous twins. I'm here to "tutor" them for an hour. The whole thing is ridiculous but it's good money and they *do* like the little quasi-academic games I make up for them.

3:50PM The twins have run through every activity I've brought them. We read books together for the next twenty-five minutes. *Anyone could do this*, I think—I think that frequently throughout my days with kids. But then their parents tell me, "I don't know how you do it!" Perhaps educating small children with love and patience actually *is* a skill, contrary to what our culture teaches about "women's work"? I wonder about various feminist theories on child-rearing while reading rhymes in a silly voice.

4:15PM My jobs are done. I'm walking to the train. At home, I know, my daughter and husband are waiting, and all my little obligations line up behind them. The dishes to be done, lessons to plan, meals to cook, gifts to buy, bills to pay, travel plans to make, friends to call, toys to tidy up, book reviews to write, poems to read—all the work that makes a life.

Economic Update

Twenty-four hours is not enough to know if spontaneity is the
way to waking.

Twenty-four hours is not enough when I speak about the basis
for how I exist in reality.

Twenty-four hours is not enough to say I am beyond any
temptation to be an apologist.

Twenty-four hours is not enough to keep a historic line.

Twenty-four hours is not enough this late in human history.

Twenty-four hours is not enough for the propaganda machine to
be on and cursed.

Twenty-four hours is not enough for a foreboding to fade.

Twenty-four hours is not enough and when it is, we will stop.

Twenty-four hours is not enough of a supplication.

Twenty-four hours is not enough of a convention of time if the
hours are not possessed by us.

Twenty-four hours is not enough if the hours are ours but
ownership is not an ethos.

Twenty-four hours is not enough light and dark needed to
     besiege.

Twenty-four hours is not enough but will act as a moving force.

Twenty-four hours is not enough to fill deeply with indignation.

Twenty-four hours is not enough to shift between one under-
     standing and another.

Twenty-four hours is not enough so share the naturalness now of
     what is true.

Twenty-four hours is not enough when we are wrong and tender.

Twenty-four hours is not enough to ask with what moral
     authority can you condemn.

Twenty-four hours is not enough so we doom ourselves because
     we believe absolution is certain.

Twenty-four hours is not enough time to descend to the plains.

Twenty-four hours is not enough when a rose is incongruous.

Twenty-four hours is not enough to dwell in our real wonder.

Twenty-four hours is not enough for the profound longing that
     cannot be unfelt.

Twenty-four hours is not enough to ask: can you forego the
symbolism of the self for the self?

Twenty-four hours is not enough so you gallop on a powerful
horse for more hours than there are, toward the enemy.

Notes

Credit to Rick Wolff for the material quoted in "Economic Update (1)."

Xunantunich: A Maya ruin, also known as "Maiden of the Rock" or "Stone Woman." Once used as a ceremonial site, it is 1400 years old and lies across from the Mopan River.

Credit to Ellen Meiksins Wood's article "The Agrarian Origins of Capitalism" for some of the material in "Images for Radical Politics."

"A Most Violent Year" borrows its vocabulary from film reviews of *A Most Violent Year.*

Acknowledgments

I am so thankful to the editors of these publications for first publishing and believing in these poems, or versions of them:

Economic Update, *Third Point Press*
After, *jubilat*
My Father and I Build a Family Tree, *The Boiler*
The Robbers, *Dressing Room Poetry Journal*
Flatlands, *Divine Magnet*
Girl in Placencia, *jubilat*
At the Bar, *Word Riot*
LBD, *The Sensation Feelings Journal*
At the Gym, *The Atlas Review*
Xunantunich, *Smoking Glue Gun*
Skydeck Selfie, *Everyday Genius*
Aubade with Ham, *Word Riot*
Summer, 2014, *Pacifica Literary Review*
Images for Radical Politics, *Divine Magnet*
Institution, *Poetry Crush*
The Lady of Civilization, *Sixth Finch*; *Queen Mob's Teahouse*; *Big Lucks*
Animalia, *Divine Magnet*
Relax Melodies, *glitterMOB*
Raise, *burntdistrict*

"At Family Dinner," "At the Bar," "At the Gym," and "In West New York, NJ" appeared in the chapbook *Weekend Poems* (dancing girl press, 2014).

"Xunantunich" and "Skydeck Selfie" appeared in the chapbook *midnight blue* (Porkbelly Press, 2015).

"Summer, 2014" won Honorable Mention in *Pacifica Literary Review*'s 2015 Poetry Contest.

"The Lady of Civilization" was a finalist in Big Lucks's 2016 Best Prize Chapbook Contest for POC Poets.

*

To these people in particular whose love and labor have made this book better:

Mom, Dad, Daniela, it will always be the four of us in the small car.

Ian, for all the years.

Caryl, Danny, Sevy, and the Rescue team, my rescuers.

Christine, Mike, Heather, Miguel, Frank, Sam, Sara, Anonymous, and Ashleigh, for sharing your lives.

Crissy Van Meter, Yun Wei, Christina Drill, Connie Mae Oliver, Lee Ann Brown, Julie Agoos, Sharon Mesmer, J. Scott Brownlee, Natalie Eilbert, Brenda Shaughnessy, Jason Koo, Rosebud Ben-Oni, Amy Gall, the late Deborah Digges, my poet/writer sisters and brothers, my teachers.

Vanessa Jimenez Gabb is the author
of the chapbooks *midnight blue*
(Porkbelly Press, 2015) and *Weekend
Poems* (dancing girl press, 2014).
She received her MFA in Poetry
from CUNY Brooklyn College and
is from and lives in Brooklyn.

RESCUE PRESS